"Bija's energy comes through on every p[...] genius."

—Wayne Dyer

"With a fascinating blend of Western artistry and Eastern science, Bija Bennett explains how our breathing, like our emotion, bridges the gulf between mind and body. A useful, poetic manual for enhancing health."

—Candace B. Pert, Ph.D.
visiting professor
Center for Molecular and Behavioral Neuroscience
Rutgers University

Breathing Into Life

Breathing into Life

Recovering Wholeness Through Body, Mind, and Breath

BIJA BENNETT

A Hazelden Book
HarperCollins*Publishers*

FIRST HARPERCOLLINS EDITION PUBLISHED IN 1993

Library of Congress Cataloging-in-Publication Data

Bennett, Bija

    Breathing into life : recovering wholeness through body, mind, and breath / Bija Bennett. — 1st HarperCollins ed.

      p.   cm.

    "A Hazelden book."

    ISBN 0-06-255284-8 : $8.00

    1. Breathing exercises.   I. Title.

RA782.B46   1993   92–56189

613'.192—dc20   CIP

93 94 95 96 97 HAD 10 9 8 7 6 5 4 3 2 1

This edition is printed on acid-free paper that meets the American National Standards Institute Z39.48 Standard.

To my parents

Arlene and Marshall

for giving me

my life's breath.

Contents

• •

Acknowledgments   xi

Introduction   xiii

Breathing into Life   xv

Part I: The Power of the Breath   1

The Power of the Breath   3

Learning to Breathe   4

Our Life-Breath   6

Breathing Lessons   8

Catching Your Breath   10

Whispering Breath   12

Phrenos: The Diaphragm   14

A Daily Bath   16

The Wave   17

Pause into the Gap   20

An Interesting Conversation   21

Have You Heard?   22

A Listening Mind   24

About the Sun and the Moon   26

Sipping Breath   28

Humming Bird   29
Elevator Music   30
Row Your Boat   32
The River Flows   34
Jazz   35
Your Own Graduate Course   36

Part II: Recovering Wholeness   39

Just Breathe   41
Profound Attunement   42
Being There   44
Reach in the Dark   46
A Sunrise   48
Being Lazy   50
Holding On   52
In a Cage   54
Raw Breath   55
Crying   56
On the Edge   58
The Lotus and the Mud   60
A Wake-Up Call   61
Feeling Intelligent   62
Absolute Uncertainty   64
Wet, Wild, and Windy   66
It Takes Heart To Breathe   68
Experience the Observer   69
Dive Deep   70

Part III: Catching the Spirit of Breath   73

Secret Spirit   75
Fresh Breezes   76
Return to the Well   77
Yawning   78
Falling   79
Currents   80
A Wavy Sea   81
Ride the Waves   82
Ode to the Tide   84
The Disappearing Act   85
A Circle Game   86
Opposites Attract   87
Best Friends   88
A Butterfly's Wings   89
Social Dance   90
Global Breath   91
Stellar Songs   92
Who Is It?   93

About the Author   95

Acknowledgments

I would like to express my love and deep appreciation to all the teachers and friends who inspired and supported me in the creation of this book. I especially wish to thank Maharishi Mahesh Yogi for giving me the gift of self-referral consciousness. Heartfelt thanks to my friend and mentor Dr. Deepak Chopra, who has always believed in my vision.

Grateful thanks to my yoga teachers T.K.V. Desikachar and Gary Kraftsow for sharing their profound knowledge on the art of breathing. Thanks to Andy Caponigro, whose insights into the healing properties of the breath have powerfully influenced my work. And to my dear friends Dr. Jacob Liberman and Donald Glenn Theiss, whose love and attention helped me to move deeply into the process of my own healing.

Loving thanks to my agent and friend, Lynn Franklin, who has encouraged and advised me for years. To Rose Brandt, whose close friendship supported me through both the hair-raising and blissful stages of writing this book. And finally to my editor, Judy Delaney, who saw my potential as a writer and carefully nurtured my growth.

Introduction

• •

Thousands of years ago the great Eastern sages
discovered that breath tapped directly into the link
between man and nature, between body and
mind. These discoveries evolved into a science
that was used to heal the body-mind, optimize
health, increase longevity, dissolve fear, and develop
higher states of consciousness.

Breathing is the expression of life, the pulsation of all that exists.
Everything in creation *breathes*—it is in the movement of the stars,
the planets, the earth, the ocean waves, the wind in the trees.
These impulses, these frequencies, these rhythms of creation, are
expressions of the universal breath of life. This living breath is the
same breath that exists within our own bodies.

Breath is the fundamental link between all things in nature. It is
our conscious relationship to life. Breathing connects our awareness
to every movement, every thought, every emotion we have. How
we breathe is how we live. And the way we breathe can allow us to
recover our wholeness, our balance of body and mind. Creating a
living balance simply means restoring our *memory of wholeness*,
connecting us back to the source of our consciousness. Our breath

keeps us in contact with this source, uniting our individual life with all of life.

As we learn to reawaken the natural flow of our breath, we begin to heal ourselves and return to wholeness. By using the breath to move our attention within the body, we explore the ever-shifting flow of energy that creates our inner experience. We begin to develop a conscious familiarity with ourselves. We begin to discover the powerful intelligence that is already breathing within us. We begin *Breathing into Life*.

This book is about breathing, but it is not a technical book or simply a collection of exercises. Let it be a personal book about your life and your breath. Let it be inspirational and meditative. Use it as a tool for self-exploration. Allow it to be a companion as you learn to open your awareness, heal your emotions, and get in touch with the rhythms of your body.

As you read, you will become more aware of your breathing. But you really don't have to think about it. You just have to be with your breath, follow it easily, and allow it to change. And as you experience the natural flow of your breathing you will notice that everything else in your life begins to move more freely.

Many of these pieces can be used as exercises. But be playful with them. Do what appeals to you. There is no goal to achieve. Just be easy with yourself and your own breath will lead the way. Pick up the book and open it anywhere. It is for you to use in any way you wish.

Breathing into Life

Most likely
    if you
            happen
to fall into a lake
            you may
                    remember to breathe
and
 for a moment
            fully appreciate
        your life
                and your breath.

I

The Power of the Breath

The Power of the Breath

The breath is remarkable.

You can learn a lot from the breath. It is profoundly wise.

It's true that every emotion, physical condition, resistance, disturbance, or tension you have is connected to your breath.

Do you ever notice that you are holding your breath? Remember what you do when you are afraid, or tense, or worrying about something? Or how your breath is when you are feeling happy? Or sad? Or when you've been sitting at your desk all day?

It's the breath that is carrying the message.

The breath can be your best friend. It can be a tool to balance, release, and free your mind and body. It can bring you strength and courage. It can calm you down or give you energy.

Breathing is an art.
But you don't need to be taught *how* to breathe.

Breathing needs not to be taught, but liberated.

Gentle, conscious, flowing, moving—

the power of the breath.

[3]

Learning to Breathe

● ●

But you already know how to breathe!
        Breathing is one of those things
you don't ever have to think about like hearing or seeing, isn't it?
        Yes. Absolutely.
   You can go through your whole life and never give your
breathing another thought.
        Maybe that's why it hardly ever occurs to you
that you are not breathing maximally
        or getting the most out of your breath.

   Attention to your breath
can make it possible to access the real potential
                in almost any area of your life.
Your breath can
   maximize your energy, strengthen your immunity, increase
your circulation, align your posture, promote relaxation,
improve your digestion and elimination, reduce pain and fear,
help to focus your attention
   and much, much more.

The best part is, it doesn't cost anything to
experience all of this.

Learning to breathe comes naturally
by eavesdropping
on
the moment-to-moment flow of consciousness in your body
through the moment-to-moment
flow of your breath.

Then you can access
the unlimited
information, energy, and intelligence
within
that guides you
through the process of your life.

Our Life-Breath

In the ancient yogic texts
  it is said
that breath is the life force. As long as there is breath in the
body,
    there is life.
        Life is breath and breath is life.
    They call this life force *Prana*.
Each of your body's functions
    has its own life-breath, or *prana*. There is one in the brain,
one in the head and chest, one in the throat and lungs, one in
the stomach, one in the lower abdomen, and one that circulates
throughout the entire body.

  *This means that everything you do, say, think, or feel
      is intimately connected to your breath.*

    Your breath touches everything.
    It vibrates in every cell of your body.
It enables your mind to think, your eyes to see, your skin to feel,
    your mouth to speak, your food to be digested,
        and your body to perform all functions.

    Breath is truly the *nectar of life*.

The scriptures say that contemplation of *prana,* or breath,
bestows longevity and self-knowledge on all those who are
devoted to its practice.
    They tell us that
the impurities of one's heart and mind are destroyed
        bringing health, happiness, and freedom from disease.

        (Not bad for just breathing some air.)

    All this really means
is that when you let go of your resistances
        and allow yourself to be open to the rhythms of your breath
                your whole life changes.
    Your system expands, rotates
                    and radiates like a wheel of light.
        It throws off an entirely new energy.
                    Not one of separate parts
                    but one of wholeness.
    Then you start deeply connecting and joyfully relating
            to all the infinite possibilities
                along the journey
                    of your life
                        and your breath.

Breathing Lessons

Remember
this is not a breathing class.
This is your breath
and this is your life.
No one is going to judge you, test you
or give you a grade.

So let's get honest about where your breath is right now.

Do you feel yourself straining as you inhale?
Notice any resistance. And take your time.
Allow your exhale to become a little longer and slower.
Don't let the out-breath release too fast.
Notice if you collapse your body as you breathe out. Instead,
feel a slight contraction of your belly as you exhale slowly.

Let your breathing become smooth and easy.
And just keep watching your breath.

You can keep your eyes open and even continue reading
as you breathe in and out easily
and effortlessly.

Stay with your breath for a moment.

You can even close your eyes and just be with your self
and your breath. It's okay to put the book down.

Give your breath some freedom again.
Feel what is going on inside you right now.
Notice your thoughts. Notice what you are feeling.

Stay with your breath.

And let the flow of your breath
lead you
to your present state of energy and awareness.

There is nothing you need to do.
Just allow your awareness to be with your breath.

Listen.

And respect yourself.

Then you will see that everything you are looking for

is right there.

Catching Your Breath

· ·

What happens
          when you are
out of breath?
          You pant
gasping
     for air
          trying to *catch your breath*
     as if it was lost
               and needed to be found.

Find your breath
          and use it wisely.

Because once you start paying attention to your feelings
                    once you *come to your senses*
     and begin to breathe
          consciously and presently

     the energy of life courses through you.

     This is the gift that life has given you.

You don't have to be confused.
You don't have to think about how it could or couldn't be.
Just live.
Just be.
Just *breathe*.

Catching your breath
is what happens
when you find yourself.
When you discover
that you're
totally here
and alive.

Whispering Breath

When you breathe
                    you can breathe
through your *nose*
            or your *mouth*
                        or from the back of your *throat*.

Try something for a moment.

            Whisper the word "ha."
And listen to where this breath originates
                in your throat.
Now close your mouth
        breathe through your nose
            and create this same soft

            whispering sound
that comes when you breathe
            from the back of your throat (without vocalizing).
                    It sounds smooth and light.
        A rushing sound
                like *the wind through the trees*.
                Both on inhale
                        and exhale

keep this air-sound

       sounding

         softly.

    Slow, deep, and steady
      inhalations
and exhalations.

    Listen to the sound of your breath.

Let the air do it for you.
And be easy. There is no need to force it in or out.
    Just keep it smooth. Very smooth.

This sound-like breathing
   is an ancient technique
that helps you

        to expand, lengthen, and deepen your breath.
     It's calming. And invigorating.

   Allow yourself a few minutes to try it.
      Close your eyes.

    And just breathe.

Listen to this
    smooth, soft, even
      whispering sound of your breath.

Phrenos: The Diaphragm

The diaphragm
        is the central muscle of the human body.
The principal muscle
        of your breath.
In ancient Greece the diaphragm was phrenos—
        the unity of all possibilities of human expression
           —the link between body, mind, and breath.

The dome-like diaphragm is so strategically located
           it is said to be a work of art.
    Your heart rests over it.
Your liver and spleen lie below it. It's attached to your spine.
    As it moves
        it encloses and touches all your abdominal organs.
        The diaphragm interconnects
your heart, your abdomen, your lungs, and your spine.
    And because of these relationships
        its movement profoundly affects
your posture, digestion, elimination, and respiration.
        This is your diaphragm
      the mediator of all rhythms
        biological and emotional.

The rhythmic movement of your diaphragm
is changing constantly.
Relaxed
it is shaped like a dome
arching into the cavity of your chest.
As you inhale it contracts down, pressing on your organs
and opening up your chest.
Air rushes in as you breathe.
As you exhale your diaphragm relaxes. Rising.
Pushing the air up and out.

The diaphragm swings
as you breathe.
Rising and falling. Relaxing and contracting.
The air is drawn into your lungs and expelled.
Naturally breathing, pumping, continually massaging
your organs, heart, and lungs. Ebbing and flowing.
A never-ending movement.
All one movement.
United with what you feel
with what you say
with what you breathe.
So free your diaphragm.
Let it move. Let it feel. And let it breathe.
Phrenos. Unifying all possibilities of body, mind, and breath.

A Daily Bath

Every movement of your spine
is connected in some way to your breath.
Notice that if you slump even slightly
your lung capacity is diminished.
But when your spine is long and free
you expand the cavity of your chest
so that more air can pass in and out.
Your posture and breath
are intimately linked. They profoundly affect one another.

Through your breath you speak to your spine.

All breathing, all movement, is good for your spine.
It brings a flow of nutrients and fluids to your discs.
Focus deeply inside for a moment
and see that both your inhale and exhale
initiate a lively response in your spine. Take a long, slow
breath in and notice how your spine lengthens and extends.
Your inhale creates a stretching and expanding of your spine.
When you exhale notice how your spine rounds at its base.
Your exhale creates a bending or flexion in your lower back.

It feels great to *give your spine a daily bath* while you breathe.

The Wave (A Basic Breath for Healing and Awareness)

• •

Practice *The Wave* one step at a time for several breaths.
Move on to the next step as you feel ready.

I. *Awareness*

Sit quietly for a moment
with your eyes closed.
Let your back lengthen and widen
as you delicately release through the back of your neck.

Fill your body
with your awareness.

Begin to deepen your breath.
And notice
that as you shift your attention
to your breath
your posture begins to change.
Feel the natural relationship
between your breath
and the movement of your spine

Continue
and observe.

II. *Movement*

Now notice
    that as you inhale
        and fill your upper chest first
      your spine naturally lengthens and extends.
It rises and expands as you breathe in slowly and easily.
      When you exhale
    your spine softens
      moving back into the center of your body
as your lower back rounds.
While breathing out
    gradually tighten your belly and move it towards your spine.
Keep noticing
    the wave-like motion of your spine
        as you continue breathing.
    Inhaling and exhaling.

      Stay with the rhythm of your breath.

III. *Breath*

When you begin your next inhale
      notice that your diaphragm moves downwards
        allowing the air
          to be drawn in and down.

And when you exhale, notice that your diaphragm moves up
pushing the air up and out.
The inhale moves in and down. The exhale moves up and out.

As your diaphragm moves
your breath moves.
And as your breath moves
your spine moves.

Continue
and breathe.

Through this smooth, gradual, and even flow
of your breath
your body is released back
into its natural motion.

The Wave

It's a magnificent motion of your breath.

Pause into the Gap

Come back
    into that deep, smooth whispering sound
of your breath. And as you continue breathing
                        notice that there is a
    pause
            between each breath.
This natural
        effortless
        pause
    is the moment of stillness
            or gap
    that comes before the next breath begins.
Every breath is born
            out of this pause
                    between inhale and exhale
    and between exhale and inhale.
            It arises, unfolds, and disappears
                into the gap.

Find this space. Hear the silence.
    And pause
            into the gap.

An Interesting Conversation

* *

Your breath
       is a communications center.
   It helps you
          to remain awake
and aware.

       Hello. Are you there?

    Smooth, easy inhale.
Longer, slower exhale.
       Whispering so you can hear.

    Body, mind, and breath. All lines connect.

Now
   listen
to the never-ending conversation
      of your breath.

Have You Heard?

• •

Have you heard
      the song
      and silence
      of your breath?

There is music inside your body.

Yes, music.
Sit down and get ready for a musical performance.
    (You might read this first and then follow along.)

Shut both eyes carefully with your fingers.
    Close your mouth
        and cover your ears with your thumbs.
            (If you can't see or hear, that's the idea.)

Begin to create some long, slow
        inhalations and exhalations.
            And listen to the song of your breath.
Listen for the sounds
        and the silences.
            Pay attention to the pauses between each breath.

What do you hear?

     Notice the melodies
     flowing inside your body.
Keep breathing.
    And listening. (Beethoven would have loved this.)

     You are the maestro.
      You are guiding your awareness
     and your breath.

     Have you heard?

New music. New listening.
Not an attempt to understand something.
     Just an attention
       to the
         sounds
       and silences
       of your breath.

Simply listen
to the music inside your body.
       Because
         everybody has a song.

A Listening Mind

Paying attention
is not a narrowing-down process
    or a discipline
of your mind.
Paying attention
    is an experience of freedom.
        It is having a listening mind.

Let yourself
 become aware of your breath for a moment
    and notice
any feelings of discomfort in your body.
    And at the same time
    notice
that the sun is shining
        and the dog is barking
    and that the people in the next room are talking.
        Keep breathing
and notice
    that all of this
        is happening
            in a remarkable relationship

between you, your breathing,
and all you are observing.

Open your focus of attention
and stay with your breath.
Listen.
And notice that an amazing thing happens.

Your world opens up.

It becomes a world that is not narrow
or restricted.
But a world that is full of discoveries
moment to moment.
Paying attention is what happens
when you have a listening mind,
when you stay with your breath and observe
what is going on inside you and around you.
And if you are totally open to this experience
then everything
becomes
extraordinary.

Life becomes interesting and alive.

About the Sun and the Moon

● ●

There is a real relationship between
your nostrils and your entire physiology.
Nasal breathing alters the cortical activity of the brain
and corresponds to the dominance of the brain's
left or right hemispheres.
So breathing through each nostril
influences body chemistry in a special way.

The left nostril conducts *cooling* energy to the body and mind
stimulates the right hemisphere
and in the ancient scriptures is associated with *the moon*.

The right nostril conducts *heating* or warming energy
stimulates the left hemisphere and is associated with *the sun*.

Predominately breathing through one nostril or the other
creates a specific effect.

For cooling with the moon:
Close your right nostril with your right thumb.
Inhale through your left nostril. Slowly, deeply, and fully.
Close your left nostril with the ring and little fingers.
Exhale right nostril.

Repeat this for a few moments. Inhale left. Exhale right.
Feel the cooling throughout your system.
Continue to breathe smoothly and easily.

For warming with the sun:
Close your left nostril with the ring and little fingers
of your right hand.
Inhale through your right nostril. Slowly, deeply, and fully.
Close your right nostril with your right thumb.
Exhale left nostril.
Repeat this for a few moments. Inhale right. Exhale left.
Feel the warming throughout your system.
Continue to breathe smoothly and easily.

Left. Moon. Cooling.
Helps to calm the mind. Regulates anger. Eases insomnia.
Cools an overheated body. Reduces restlessness and stress.

Right. Sun. Heating.
Promotes digestion—good before eating. Increases energy.
Enhances mental focus and concentration.
Enlivens the body for physical activity.

This is how you can use
*the rising and the setting of the sun and moon
in your own life.*

Sipping Breath

It's cooling
this breath.
Like *sipping* lemonade on a hot sunny day.

Pretend you are sipping through a straw as you inhale.
Make sure you hear the sound (like a hiss) as you sip.
Then close your mouth
and exhale using the *Whispering Breath*
from the back of your throat.
Repeat this for a few breaths.
Sipping on inhale through your mouth.
Exhaling from the back of your throat, mouth closed.

Feel the wind and the moisture
that is brought into your breath as you inhale.

Close your eyes. And allow your spine and your head
to move like a gentle wave. You are circulating wakeful, refreshing
energy through your body as you breathe.

A sipping breath.

Cooling and soothing for your body and mind.

Humming Bird

Humming birds *hum*.
Notice
that when you *hum*
it resonates in your
head, chest, and throat.
Inhale completely through your nose
and as you exhale
produce a humming sound.
Keep humming (in one tone) until you need to inhale
again.
Repeat this for a minute or so. Close your eyes
and feel how and where the sound vibrates in your body.
Pause after you exhale and notice the silence.
Breathing slowly, softly.
Soothing every cell.

Humming birds *hum*.
A calming
easing
healing
sound
for your body and mind.

Elevator Music

. . . .

You know what it's like
    to go down an elevator
        and stop at every floor.
There's a breathing practice
    that uses this same technique.
      You breathe
        in stages.
          In steps.
Like this.
    Exhale, then pause. Exhale, then pause. All in one out-breath.
Then inhale and do it again.
    Exhale in stages
      with two pauses in between.
Try it again.
    Then add a step. Now the elevator stops on three floors
      before it goes all the way down.
    Exhale, pause. Exhale, pause. Exhale, pause.

    Be aware of *The Wave*. Close your eyes.
    And really *feel* your breath. Breathe slowly.
    Hearing the sounds and the silences of your breath.

Your exhale moves like a wave from the bottom up.
    It's a soft gathering at your base
        as your belly moves towards your spine.

Your inhale moves like a wave from the top down.
    Fill your chest and expand your ribs
        as you inhale easily, effortlessly.

Elevator music.

It's calming. It helps you to extend
    and therefore quiet your breath.
Add some more floors.
    Step by step.
        Moving with your breath
          down to the bottom floor.

Mind still.
Breath still.

Row Your Boat

* *

Row, row, row your boat
  gently down the stream. You remember that song.
    Singing is breathing. Try it.
Try taking a deep breath in
   and as you exhale
     sing (or say) the first two lines of the song.

Then inhale
  breathing through your nose
   and try it again. Always singing the line
as you exhale.
     Come on, it's fun!
If that was easy
  add the next two lines to make your exhale even longer.
    Merrily, merrily, merrily, merrily
     life is but a dream.
Do the whole thing, or build up gradually
  to all four lines on one exhale without pausing for a breath.
   Then inhale and repeat it again.
Now remember *The Wave.* Feel your belly contract as you exhale.
   And expand your chest on inhale.

This is a breathing practice.
Do it consciously. Smoothly. Evenly.
(Almost any song will do.)

The slower you do it, the more you need to pace your breath.

Singing
or chanting
when used as a breathing practice
circulates the energy in your body
and controls the flow of your breath.
It opens up your throat
focuses your attention
and deeply stimulates your entire system.

See if you can feel some increased warmth
some vibration
some change of the feelings inside
as you vocalize
and breathe.

Let your whole body begin to sing.

Did you ever think
that boating (or breathing)
could be so much fun?

The River Flows

Continue to come back to your breath
  and it will become smoother and smoother.
 Then comes spontaneity
  when your breath just moves as it wishes.

  It is just as when bathing in a river.
At first, you swim by your own strength.
   But once you are caught in the current
   you are simply carried away.

  Enter the rhythms of your breath.
    Listen and feel what it wants to be.
Then you will see
  that everything proceeds along smoothly and spontaneously.

You know when you have surrendered to your breath.
    There are signs.
You feel a deep sense of delight,
    a feeling of release and exhilaration.

  Go with the currents of your breath

    and get carried away.

Jazz

Think of your breath *as jazz*.
And you can improvise
    starting with some fast breaths.
            Some rapid, *soft,* and punchy breaths.
Quick eighth notes of breath. Breathing through your nose.
            Accenting on the exhale.
Finish with some longer, slower, deeper *whispering breaths*.
    Lyrical, light, airy-sounding breaths.
            Then deeper, peaceful, wave-like breaths.

            Awareness of spontaneity.
                Not choreographed.
        But lively, rhythmical, improvisational breaths.
            This is jazz. Many variations. Let yourself go.
Feel what kind of breath is being breathed.
            Could be a bebop-breath
            a swing-like breath
            a waltzing-kind-of-breath.
Original melodies. Always remembering
        that you can never breathe the same breath
            in the same way ever again.
    Just let it happen. Let it be amazing. And breathe. *Jazz*.

Your Own Graduate Course

• •

You know
    this practice of breathing isn't new.
It's an ancient body of knowledge
    that has been studied for thousands of years.
Pranayama
the yogic art and science of breathing
    develops
awareness
      of the infinite combinations
    created by your breath.
      You can breathe through your nose
      your mouth
      through the back of your throat.
You can inhale
exhale
and pause
    in so many
      different designs
patterns
      and
    arrangements.

[36]

(Already
you have become a dedicated student
       of this science.)

So keep studying and exploring
              and discover
    a constellation of possibilities
for your life's
    breath.

II

Recovering Wholeness

Just Breathe

Hey You!

Where are you? And what do you feel?

You are not a helpless
    victim
of your emotional states.
    If you'd like your emotions
        to move through you

just breathe.

Profound Attunement

Merely putting your awareness
    in your body
        and breathing
is a process of
        healing.
    Did you know that there is a real relationship
between the quality of your attention
        and the capacity to heal yourself?
    When you have an alert appreciation
      of what's really going on
within you
    and outside you
        something inside
           begins to express itself.
When you start paying attention
        to your feelings
    to your body
      and to your breath
  something inside
        begins to tell you what you need.

    Healing is profound attunement.

Close your eyes and feel the silence.
   Tune in and allow your awareness
to flow through your entire body.
      Notice what is there.
Maybe you feel some sensation somewhere.
Maybe you feel some emotion
      welling up
         inside.
            Begin to breathe. Allow whatever comes
            to just happen.
There is no need to change or manipulate anything. *Just be there*
   with whatever is there.
            Discover
            where your awareness goes.
   And feel what you feel.
            Simply appreciate yourself.
Open yourself to yourself. *And breathe.*
   If you are willing to *tune in*
      you will find that the energy of your awareness
can change you deeply. Because *profound attunement*
      is the natural state of healing and transformation.
         Open yourself and participate.

            Listen
               to your life.

Being There

When you feel so frustrated
       that you are getting yourself all wound up,
rather than letting it shake you and break you, take this energy
       and do something with it.

You are feeling this energy intensely
       and you feel the tension inside yourself.
Just keep watching it and being present with it.
(This is the hardest thing to do.) Because these tensions are
powerful.

And if you stay with them
       and begin to breathe into them
         and channel them
you attend to the stages in the flow of energy as it changes
       from something dense to something really moving.
(It doesn't happen immediately.)
       So really remain with yourself and be patient.

And when you think you can't stand it anymore
remember to take another breath (keep moving your breath)

and bring your attention really deep inside you,
that means really deep inside.
Find your breath
and let it help you, since it is your best friend.

Trust yourself
and your ability to create this change
that is taking place
and notice as you feel this change
that whatever you are thinking about or feeling so intensely
also changes. (You are growing.)
And when you attend to yourself like this
again and again
you start to notice more clearly that

when you resist something in your life, there is tension
and that when you let go, there is flow.

It really is exactly the same energy pulsating within you
and unfolding into all forms of your experience.

Reach in the Dark

It's really hard to see sometimes
when you reach into the depths of your emotional pain.
Things aren't clear
        and seem unbearable
           to face.
But how do you overcome something when you are there alone
    in the dark?

    When the door seems shut and wants to be unlocked?

Listen to the sound of your breath and notice that even
        the smallest breeze

      can get you to feel again.

 As you inhale ever so gently
        feel how the breath frees your spine
               and allows the energy to circulate.

      There is no need to force it in
        just open the door.

As you exhale

    gradually move your belly towards your spine.

        You don't need to work very hard. Just stay present.

Feel the strength of your base

    as you release your breath

slowly

    and firmly.

        Continue breathing

        and reach into the dark.

Soon you'll begin to feel some deep and healing silence

        coming in

like light

    shining through the crack in the door.

A Sunrise

Are you afraid to be with yourself
              when you feel deeply hurt?

    You might be holding out for someone
        to fix it and make it better. Someone
            to acknowledge your pain.

    You can acknowledge *yourself*
    as you observe how and when you shut yourself down.
Or how and when you go weak.
    Or how and when you criticize and judge yourself.

Being good to yourself in the midst of your pain is a challenge.
And you can start by recognizing where in your body
    you feel it most. Because in order to change something

        you need to observe it
            bring it to the light

and not push away, deny, or resist the fact

that it is there
        inside.

And then a little breathing makes a big difference.

In truth, it really doesn't matter why you got stuck.
      The darkness is still dark.

Know that by deeply connecting to the feelings inside
      and by *listening to your breath*

you can get out of the way of yourself
      so something wise can take over.

You can actually
      get out of your own way

      and allow the sun to rise.

Being Lazy

Do you think that you are
being lazy
    when you are not *doing* something?
Do you think that you are
wasting your time
      when you are simply
          just being there?
   There's nothing wrong
with just sitting still and watching.
Maybe real laziness
is when
    your mind is unaware of its own reactions.
Or when you're not paying attention to what is going on
    inside you.

      This is when you're really asleep.

Quite frankly
    your restless mental wanderings
        have nothing to do with
           knowing or learning anything.

However
if you allow yourself
to be watchful
of the trees
or the wind
or the people
or your breath
you can make some *brilliant discoveries*.

Using your breath is most convenient.

It is always there
and it immediately leads you
to the knowledge of what is happening
right now.
This is good to know.

For when the next time comes
that you are frantically pushing
or frustrated
or working all day to achieve what you want

you can get a little lazy

and just watch yourself
and
your breath.

Holding On

● ●

Do you hold your breath when you're afraid?

It could be
that you're driving down the highway in icy weather
or
flying in an airplane (and it isn't all that smooth)
or
thinking about that delicate conversation you've got to have.
By this time
    you know
it really doesn't help to hold your breath.

    But let's try something for a moment.

On the count of three, take a big, deep breath in. *And hold it*.
        Keep holding.
        Keep holding.
        Keep holding.

    Feels pretty tight.
        Not too relaxing, is it?

Notice what's happening right now. Be aware of your feelings
    in relation to your breath.
You know
    breath and fear are intimately connected.

When you get scared or anxious
    you tend to protect yourself
    block your energy
    and hold on.
And sometimes you don't even know you're doing it.
    (Okay, you can let it go now.)

    Maybe
when you're afraid
instead of holding your head up high and whistling a happy tune
    you could try a little breathing.
Steady, smooth, back-of-the-throat-sounding breathing.
That's right.
    Keep it going. And be courageous.

        You'll simply watch your fear and tension
          lose its holding on.

In a Cage

Like a bird
    in a cage
you hold your breath.
Maybe you think
    that if you hold on (to it)
                a little more
you won't lose it (whatever *it* is).
It could be anything—feelings, tensions, fears.
Maybe you can even
control it
        if you hold on (to it).
Don't be that poor bird
    in a cage. (You can't breathe.)
When you release
 or let go of what resists inside you
        and you hear the wings of your breath flutter
           you feel freedom.
        Keep your body moving and breathing. Stay fully alive.
There is always further and
               further
                    to fly.

Raw Breath

Touch the raw parts of yourself
                with your breath.
Feel the edges of your system
          that are strained
                  or exhausted.
      Appreciate your tiredness.

What makes all the difference
          is accepting what is going on.

Envelop yourself with awareness.
      Include every cell.
Expand beyond the corners of your fingers and limbs.
In every direction
      let your attention
            open and expand the feeling inside your body.

      Like a blanket
            cover yourself
      entirely
            with your breath.

Crying

Remember how babies cry?
> They take a big deep breath
> > and let out a
> > > *huge wail.*
> They don't hold back. They just let go.
> *Loudly.*

And sound out their breath.
> > Long, long exhale cries. Then short, fast, inhale sobs
> > as they begin to quiet down (maybe).

It's natural to cry.
> And it doesn't mean that you are weak.

It means you are strong enough to take the risk of letting go.

> Sobbing
> is the most powerful and genuine release in your system.
> > It frees you and cleanses you.
> It cleans out your emotions, it cleans out your thoughts
> > and it cleans out your body.
> > Ever notice how you feel after you cry?

It's like a river running through.

The next time you cry you'll probably appreciate your breath.
Allow it to support you and keep you present
with your feelings.

Give yourself permission to cry
like a child.

Because
when you open yourself up
your breath flows more easily through your system.
It rearranges your whole inner structure.

It's okay.

Let yourself go and cry.

Sob, scream, sniff, and sigh.

On the Edge

• •

There is a part of you that
    needs to know what's going to happen
    before you do anything.
The part of you that wants to be safe and predictable.

The truth is that being really open to yourself
is not predictable. It is not safe.

      It is on the edge.

If you try to control the outcome of anything—
      people, places, and things—
you may get control of the form but you destroy the substance.
You lose the joy of responding to the creative energy of your life.

    All holding on, all forms of control
    originate in your body with your breath.

When you are afraid, you protect, grab, or push away.
    You do the same thing with your breath.
    Watch yourself sometime. When this happens (and it will)
tune in to the network of your tightness.
    Watch your breathing.
And notice how tense your body feels when you try to control.

Note the disturbance inside and be with it.
Move into it and allow it.

It's true *you don't know where anything will lead you.*

Maybe you could fall off the cliff. Maybe you could fly.
Let the discomfort build.
Be real with what is there.
Observe your inhale and exhale
and be gentle as you guide your breath to deeper levels.
The feelings may even escalate.
Surround yourself with your awareness.
Accept your turmoil, uncertainty, or fear. Get in there with it.
But don't lose track of your breath.
Watch the parts of your body that feel irritated, frustrated, or hurt.
Where are you most uncomfortable? Remain with your breath.

You may feel like sighing or even sobbing.
It's just the pressure that wants to be released.
Let yourself go. *You are actually more secure when you let go.*

Stay on the edge.

That's where your life is. That's where your breath is.

The Lotus and the Mud

When you become involved in your strain
    tension
        or fear
            you get stuck in it
                like walking through river mud.
But when you can take a breath
    and draw these feelings to a different point
    within you
then these feelings begin to release.
    They change. And you awaken to something new.
And when you awaken to something new
           you begin to move and your energy starts to flow.
    You look at the event and respond to what it has to say.
You're not avoiding it, or covering it up.
    You are moving it.
        Moving your consciousness.
This can free your energy. *And your life.*

      It changes your focus
            and allows you to grow.

(And as you know, lotus flowers grow out of the mud.)

A Wake-Up Call

Stop
and notice where you are
this moment.
        Are you available to yourself?
Can you see
where
        you are *not?*
Come on and be here right now.
        Jump into present-moment awareness.
And notice your breath.
        Is it short?
        Is it shallow?
                Does it gradually get deeper when you
                stay with it a little while longer?
        Maybe you think this is terribly boring.
Or you don't have time for just some breathing.
                But it's amazing
                        how often you are asleep
to the power and knowing *of your own presence.*
And how even a casual reminder can open your eyes to
        something entirely different.

Feeling Intelligent

Who said that thinking
        is about being intelligent?

        Read, think, and make yourself
clever. Does it bring you freedom? Yet you always head for it.
    Proud of your authority, rules, and self-control.
        Can't you see?

True intelligence
        is
    the ability
        to feel, touch, taste, smell, hear, and see
           what is really there
                inside.

Use your breath
        simply
           to feel.

Acknowledge
    your aliveness

right now.
Listen to your breath.
There is nothing more present
more intelligent
than your breath.
Don't be a fool.
Be wise.
It's not in the details.
But in the moment
now.

It takes *tremendous intelligence*
to breathe
feel
and be real
from wherever you are.

Absolute Uncertainty

● ●

Certainty.
That really means
    inevitable result
    foregone conclusion
    and sure thing.

        If you ever feel uncertain in your life
you grab for something to hold on to
                that feels certain.

    When you desire certainty in your life
        you *fix* yourself on an outcome
    or *hold on* to a given boundary.

    Notice how this fixing and holding *feel* in your body.
Find out what would it be like to go deep inside
        and just breathe for a moment.

    Lower the bucket into the well and see what comes up.
Feel the breath surrounding the tension of your grasp.
      It's true that letting go is frightening.

But so what?
Trust yourself.
Break the boundaries
and
dive into absolute uncertainty.
Throw it
all into the air
with your breath.

Because whatever you really need will come back
and whatever you don't
will just
drift
away.

Wet, Wild, and Windy

When you look at waves
                    from a distance
                              they almost look
        still.

Get right down in there
            and they are deep
                        and daring.
One
        right after the other.
                    Breaking
                              wildly

                              turbulent

        with abandon,
            with meaning.

Your feelings,
            when you don't look at them,
                              when you hide
from a distance,
            they seem to disappear. And all that is left
            are your mind-born waves

from where you cease to feel.
Don't be afraid to feel.

Drop yourself into
your raging-waves.
You can ride them.

You can cross the sea.
It's unfathomable.

Be deep and daring.

Stay with your breathing. *And get right down in there.*

Feel what it feels like
to be tossed
around
by what you really feel.

Run to the ocean. Meet yourself there.
Many unaware ones never know
that the wet, wild, and windy waves
that feel and heal
can surely save you.
Roam
your boundless sea.

It Takes Heart to Breathe

It takes commitment
    to live from your heart. It takes patience
to come back to yourself, to believe in yourself.

    Awareness of your breath
                    opens your feelings.
            Awareness of your feelings
                    opens your heart.
    Follow your feelings to their roots.
            Your breath can take you there.
Then you may find that you feel more boundless.
Your emotions become a tremendous source of energy
  and strength.
Even the pains and anxieties that flow through you
  are opportunities to feel, sense, touch,
    and be touched by your own heart
      when it is heavy with disappointment, loneliness, or fear.
      It takes courage to let go of your pain.
But as you meet each emotion you will know that what it offers
        is the real chance to move on.
            It takes heart to breathe.

Experience the Observer

Dive deep within and discover what is real.
Whatever happens, it happens to you.
Whatever you do, the doer is you.
You are the one who is experiencing.
You are the one who is breathing. You are there inside.

Peace is the ability to be aware of what is going on inside.

Feel the difference now between your breathing, your breath,
and the one who is breathing.
If you breathe and observe
you might bump into the one who is breathing and observing.
Allow yourself this moment of inner attention.
Don't doubt yourself.

Be interested in yourself. Be intimate with yourself.
And above all, *be honest with yourself
and nothing will betray you.*

Move beyond your limitations
Return to yourself with quiet attention.
Find yourself.
And be free.

Dive Deep

* *

Don't be afraid to feel afraid.

Leave the safety of your sanctuary
and wander into something rare.
Instead of pulling away
            turn around and face it. Because whatever happens
        you won't die. (You might cry or laugh, but you won't die.)

Pay attention to what is going on inside you and
            dive deep
                        into the depths of your fear.
        Even when it feels like you are drowning
                keep the agreement with yourself
                        to go deeper. Keep breathing.
                The other side of fear is love.

Redirect your attention and change the pressure within yourself.
        Don't doubt, get discouraged, and stop the loving.
                        Feel into the feeling in your heart.
            Really breathe fully
                    and continue to let it circulate and swell.

Allow a simple love of life to emerge.

Take time with it. Go further.
Expand the currents of your breath inside you and around you.
Discover more flow.
It may well be that you need to work through a lot of tensions.
And that's all right. But the purpose is not just to work
through them
but to move beyond them.

Your breath is the vehicle that moves you through.

Diving deep
inside
you'll find
that *your love is what's really alive.*

III

Catching the Spirit of Breath

Secret Spirit

Spirit. Latin: *Spiritus*. Meaning breath.

This wind, this spirit *breathes*.
It brings forth the universe.
This wind, this spirit blows the moon across the sky
makes clouds
causes rain
germinates seeds
moves the sun and the stars
initiates the rivers and streams
and maintains all creation.
In the body
this wind, this spirit *breathes*.
It creates the structure of the body itself
regulates systems and organs
initiates all movements, all actions
coordinates the senses
and connects the mind
with the body
with the breath.
This wind, this spirit *breathes*.
It is *spiritus,* the secret breath of all life.

Fresh Breezes

Stay with yourself as your fresh emotional breezes
turn around out of nowhere.
Now, suddenly overcast, your feelings thicken like clouds
and turn to rain. Then what? Can you acknowledge them?
Let them drizzle in through your body
as you breathe.
It feels like showers pouring. Teeming sometimes. When the
storm rages around you.
In a crisis, you desperately try to control and solve it.
Your frustrations are like sleet glazing your face.
They sting. Gales blow.
But watch as then the wind veers.
Breathe, observe, and discover
how your emotions shift and move.
This warming, melting comes. Then soft soothing breezes
are stroking your skin again.
Enjoy that airy space
that breathes deeply, rhythmically within you.
The sky has cleared. Bringing renewed sensations of quiet and
calm.
Flowing in energy-air. *Your fresh breezes.*
Feel them. Breathe them.

Return to the Well

. . . .

Listen
> to the sacred sound
>> of your inward and outward
> breath.
>> The breath moves. Suspended
>> as you pause.

Drawing your breath up
> and down
>> like water from a well.

> Purifying. Body, mind, and breath.

Balancing
> the incoming and outgoing breaths
>> cultivates wholeness.

> The seat of your breath.
>> Pure inward space.

Unbounded awareness. A well of awareness.
> Return to your well.
>> *Prana.*
>>> *Life.*
> *Breath.*

Yawning

Yawning
> begins in the throat
>> stretches down
>>> lengthening
>>>> widening
>>>>> spreading
>>>>>> through the whole of
>>>>>>> your spine.

Invite a yawn.
> Let it be light and liquid. Wide then deep.

Like taking in fresh air.

It purifies you. It wakes up every cell.

A creative breath
> that dances through every fiber
>> purifying, passing through, rippling and renovating.
>>> Expressing air, space, life.

You must yawn every day.
> Because your breath moves in you
>> and like a river washes away
>>> everything that needs to be released.

> Mouth wide open. No rituals. *Simply yawn.*

Falling

Don't be afraid to use your breath.
You can treat it with respect.
But *use it*.

Let go of the leash that restrains your breath
when you hide in comfort.

You don't need to hide in comfort.

The way to stay fully alive is to keep your body moving and
breathing.
Try it. Move. Breathe.
Leap across the canyons and crevasses of your breath.

You might feel yourself falling. The truth is, it's more like flying.

Lose control.

It's a great way to breathe.

And to live.

Currents

* *

Like a hawk

fly on the currents with your breath.

Shift and adjust. Take the risk to remain present and open.

Stay with yourself. *Balance is an art.*

But you don't need to get caught up
in the confusion of your emotions
or resist them
or even think about them too much.

Just listen to them and feel them. Watch and learn from them.
Breathe into them.

Deeply.

Then
you can take off

and soar.

A Wavy Sea

In your deepest silence there is an impulse
        that moves by itself.
A natural, circulating energy.
        Undulating.
        Like the warm sea.
A *wonderful wavy sea* of wakeful breathing.
                Sometimes when you swim
        on the surface
                        you are tossed by the waves.
Those turbulent waves of mind
                                and madness.

Merge
        and
submerge into deeper breathing.
Your awareness settles
        down.
                Immersed you cease to resist.
                Surrounding. Circulating.
                        Your awareness is flowing as your breath.

Ride the Waves

. . . .

Breath
   is a series of waves.

   Impulses
of pure wakefulness
      sequentially
         unfolding in different rhythms.
   And as you turn your breath
      over and over
            you create waves
               that curve
            from inhale to exhale
                  and from exhale to inhale.
Turning and turning
      curving up, down and around
   these waves
         continually transform themselves
            again and again
                  within you.
      Self-interacting.
            Dynamic.

Your awareness
                becoming aware
                of itself.
Discover
        these waves
            that breathe within you.

Find them. Stay with them. And notice
                that the points of tension inside you
            begin to shift
                    and dissolve
                miraculously.

        It is the miracle of pure wakefulness
        in motion.

Internal waves
            let them swell
        and be silent
                    and swell again.

    Go ahead.

        Ride the waves of your breath.

Ode to the Tide

Breathing in.

Breathing out.

 And the spaces between them.

 Then
slip into the silence.
A universal pause.

The sequential unfolding of waves
 ebbing
 and
 flowing.

Remember
 the natural rhythms
  of your breath.
 Because once you are touched by these

  tides of breath

 the memory of your
wholeness
  returns.

The Disappearing Act

Disappear
    into your breath.
Advance
    and proceed
        along your way.
With every breath
    move a little further
        away
and back again.

      You are
        where you really are.
Lost
    and found
        into fullness.
Dissolve
    way, way
        into
            your breath.

A Circle Game

The breath is a continuum.
It is like a circle.
It curves when you inhale and pause
and you exhale and pause.
It arises and is born.
It perishes and it ceases.
It continues and goes on.
Round and around.
Start to stir your breath.
Start slow.
Soft.

And stir it
into motion.
Pour the inward
into
the outward breath.
And the outward
into
the inward breath.
Stir the circle of your breath.
Let it move you.

Opposites Attract

Balance
means
　　　living
　　　　　　opposites.
You can find them in your breath.
　　　　　　They breathe together.
Experience the fullness of your inhale.
　　　　　Can you expand your life in all directions?
　　　　　Exhale and see how strong you really are.
　　　　　　You are there to support yourself.

　　　　　Feeling *light and free*
　　　　　on inhale.
　　　Grounded and firm
　　　　　on exhale.
You can train yourself with your breath.
　　　Staying supple while stable. Moveable yet unmoveable.
　　　Vulnerable
　　　　　　yet
　　absolutely invincible.

Best Friends

• •

Shakily, quiveringly, quaveringly, tremblingly, shudderingly,
tremulously, flutteringly, waveringly, unsteadily, jerkily,
spasmodically, fitfully, by snatches, by fits and starts,
with a flirt and flutter
    let yourself breathe.

Easily, readily, effortlessly, simply, lightly, swimmingly,
smoothly, comfortably, softly, slowly, calmly, rhythmically,
eloquently and with pleasure
    let yourself breathe.

Wherever you are
        make friends with your breath.

A Butterfly's Wings

Everything affects everything else.
The beating of a butterfly's wings
can change tomorrow's weather.
Currents of air. Gusts that blow. Where do these masses
of flowing air come from?
When the earth rotates daily it creates
great swirls of weather. Temperatures change.
Region to region. Wind passing across deserts, lakes and oceans.
How do the mountains, the passing of the moon overhead,
or the distant stars and planets
affect our air?
A slight tremor, a breeze
ripples over mountains. Through tallest buildings.
Bridging continent to continent.
An underlying unity of nature's breath.
Everything affects everything else.
Living, breathing systems stretching across the earth and
beyond. Events that flow, breathe, and merge out of each other.
Expressions of a timeless breath. A deeper breath.
Transformations. Unfolding patterns of flowing air.

Like a butterfly's wings. Beating. Breathing.

Social Dance

● ●

Did you know that we take in 10,000,000,000,000,000,000,000
(that's 10 to the power of 22) atoms
    each time we inhale and exhale? We take in and give out
trillions and trillions of atoms continuously throughout our day.
        Air comes in and out from our body
    and meshes with the environment. This means
            that we are all intimately sharing atoms.
All the atoms that move through us
        are circulating in every living being on this planet.
        We are all breathing in each other's breath.
So it is said that sooner or later
  we will breathe an atom that has been breathed by anyone who
has ever lived before us. (Buddha, St. Francis, Groucho Marx.)
    We're all interconnected by our breath.
        Breathing is our relationship to all life.
    With breath we are no longer distinguished as separate.
        We are flowing, dancing, sharing our life, our breath
with one another.
        Breathing, circulating freely,
            smoothly from place to place, we are all
socializing as part of nature's dance.
        This social dance is our breath.

Global Breath

Add up all the breaths
    and what do you have?
                  Global Breath.

      It's marvelous!
    Every human
        animal
and plant.
    Even creatures like insects
                breathe.
Everywhere on land, air, and sea.
          The earth breathes.
    This is global breath. When every breath
              blends with every other breath.
Think about how connected we all really are.
Mix it all together.
    One.
Global Breath.

    The joy of breathing on Planet Earth.

Stellar Songs

* *

Do stars breathe?
    Sure they do.
        They expand
and contract.
            They explode
    and implode.
        That's breathing. Cosmic breathing.
    Planetary spheres surging
           twirling at lightning speeds.
The universe expands.
          Space stretches.   Widening the void.
    Particles, waves, fields *all breathing*
           serenely and silently.
    This living
      breathing
         universe is vibrant.
    Still.
    Quantum melodies,
galactic tunes of inspiration.
        Stellar songs. Full of splendor.
         Breath.

Who Is It?

. . . .

It is the breath alone
        as our conscious self
                that breathes life
      into our body.
The breath
          inside the breath.
          The one
which gives rise to everything.

How we breathe is how we live.

But who is it we spend our entire life breathing for?

Breathing into Life.
    It has no beginning or end
             but flows towards wholeness.

About the Author

∙ ∙

Bija Bennett has worked for many years developing her innovative synthesis of breath, exercise, yoga, and meditation. Her programs have helped world-famous celebrities, corporate CEOs, and thousands of others achieve serenity and health.

Bija lectures and teaches throughout the United States. Featured in the seminars of Deepak Chopra, M.D., a leader in the field of mind-body medicine, she is founding director of the Neuromuscular Integration Program at the Maharishi Ayur-Veda Health Center for Behavioral Medicine and Stress Management in Massachusetts.

For information on lectures, workshops, and private consultations, contact:

Bija Bennett
P.O. Box 396
Aspen, CO 81612